Renae Elevated:
Life, Love, and Inspiration

by

Renae Speaks

RoseDog Books
PITTSBURGH, PENNSYLVANIA 15238

RoseDog Books
585 Alpha Drive, Suite 103
Pittsburgh, PA 15238
Visit our website at *www.rosedogbookstore.com*

ISBN: 979-8-88812-297-6
eISBN: 979-8-88812-797-1

Foreword

Come along with me Renae Speaks
on this journey of healing and self-discovery.
To my mother you are my backbone.
To my father you made me strong.
Thank you to God who created me.
Thank you to my children, family, and friends
who have poured into me.
Now come watch Renae as she elevates.

Table of Contents

Elevate

Watch Renae as she elevates from the crown of her head to the soles of her feet, she cannot be beat. Now that she is on the journey to healing and self-discovery, she will not accept defeat. So, out with the old and in with the new. New life new love and happiness too. Renae, Renae was down for so long she did not have the words to say. A voice once lost has now been found so go ahead and spread the news around. Finally, has come the day when Renae will elevate.

L.R.D.

Born in June of 1985 she was so fly. Oh my, oh my that baby girl woman queen if only you knew her journey.

If only you knew the tears she cried. If only you could see her beautiful smile.

She is a woman of God who was bitter and jaded thinking she would never make it.

She is now in the process of healing and has realized the worth and value in her being.

Womanhood, motherhood, sisterhood, and faith are the paths that lead her to the ground she now stands on.

She now has her head held high and walks upright with the ability to fix her crown. Now you are probably wondering who she is well that is L.R.D. and L.R.D is me.

ME

Me is a masterpiece with two college degrees

Me is a mother and even a worker

Me can cook me can clean me can even sing

Me is a daughter me is a aunt me is a sister me is a niece

Me gave birth to life while carrying all types of emotions inside

Me can even speak two other languages

Excuse me excuse me Me is coming through I did not mean to put all this thickness on you

Just wanted to let you know that my brain is intelligent and just as sexy as my physical embodiment

Yes me is independent but can also be dependent

Me is always up on time and stay on her grind because she knows she must provide

Me is creative talkative and crazy me will have a man saying I want to have your baby

Me represents for the Queens of all races but more specifically the melanin women and girls of the world

The me that's a college student the me that's a writer the me that's a hairstylist and even a bus driver

The me that's a ballerina the me that's a gymnast the me that's a chemist and even an activist

The me that's a doctor the me that's a lawyer the me that's a janitor and even an author

The me that's a housekeeper the me that's a painter the me that's a babysitter and even a stripper

The me that's a singer the me that's a rapper the me that's a interior designer

Now I wrote these words to show my appreciation for the women like me and to let you know don't ever stop shinning you light on this world.

I am

I am creative I am amazing I am courageous and yeah I stay motivated I am strong I am a song I am a black woman Ok yeah wait hold on. I am me I am she I am we ok now who that be I am Renae Speaks A.K.A LRD I am humanity.

I realize

I realize that I am not perfect I realize that my soul is still searching I realize that I can be defensive I realize that I am scared to let someone in I realize that I have a story I realize that I am gifted I realize that I am one of God's children I realize that I placed limitations on myself I realize that my parents love me I realize that I have not let go of the ones who hurt me I realize that I tend to live in the past with the inability to move forward I realize that my greatest accomplishment was becoming a mother I realize that I am human I realize that I am beautiful

Respect my time

Please please respect my time because time is something we cannot rewind so I will respect yours and you will respect mine

Time is such a valuable commodity time is not something that is promised to be

Time should be cherished and not wasted by speaking lies, falsehoods, and fallacies

Time is something we wish we could get back when we experience a tragic event

Time does not wait for anyone so what makes you think you are the exception

Not trying to be rude just trying to get my point across if you do not respect my time you will be so at a lost

So please, please respect my time I do not know what you are trying to do with yours, but I am trying to add quality to mine

Sing

Singing is something I know God gave me as a gift and I am going to let it grow.

Girl! I did not know you could sing like that Sis I did not know you could blow but singing is all I know.

Singing makes me laugh. Singing makes me cry singing makes me feel good and warm inside.

I have been singing since I can remember, at church, school, and around the house.

But now I know that my singing is meant to take me higher and inspire.

God does not give us gifts to waste so whatever your gift is use it every day.

So, as for me and my voice I am going to sing until I can no more.

Poetry to music

I want to put poetry to music. I want to make the words come alive and leap off the paper where I write. I want to put poetry to music and sing a new tune to attract a new crowd and drive them spoken word wild. I want to put poetry to music to create a new groove and mood to reconfigure your attitude. I want to put poetry to music so we can be jumping off in this place and snap our fingers to the bass. I want to put poetry to music as an offering of praise to the most high. I want to put poetry to music so I stand on a stage and release all of me into that place. I want to put poetry to music so I can spark a thought in your mind of which poem you will hear next time.

Daddy

Daddy Daddy where did you go where were you when I needed you the most

Where were you when I needed help with my homework or even a hug or just your love

You say that there are things that I don't know about you and momma's marriage I really don't care just wanted you to be my daddy

It took having a child and getting married for you to step up and try to be in my life

I thought that there was something wrong with me because it was easier for you to be a grandaddy than a father to me

I was so busy trying to find a man that was not like you that my marriage was doomed from the start I never really gave my heart I was just waiting for the other shoe to drop

Because daddy what you taught me is that men are inconsistent and at some point, they will lie cheat and leave you in the distance

But daddy you also taught me how to grind and be a hustler no matter how many times in and out of jail you always found a job and had consistent income

I keep hoping that you will break the cycle and be there for your grandkids, but your granddaughter is almost grown now so we see that is a fail

Daddy, I know this may hurt your heart but I really had to get my feelings all out

So, I can heal and now reveal that I forgive you and the love I have is real.

The man who broke my heart

The man who broke my heart is loving and crazy. Everytime he calls I hear "hey baby". The man who broke my heart was inconsistent and though that I cared about his finances. The man who broke my heart did not understand that all I really needed was his presence. The man who broke my heart would have me waiting only to see the sunset fade into darkness. The man who broke my heart moved around a lot but always managed to have a good job. The man who broke my heart made me question the motives of every man who showed interest. The man who broke my heart has made me feel loved and also carry resentment. The man who broke my heart was my father.

Friend

Friend Friend Friend where do I began like writing a term paper for college trying to find a middle and an end.

Friend is loving

Friend is kind

Friend is smart

Friend be on her grind

Friend is inspiration friend be giving me all types of motivation

Friend is bold, sexy, beautiful, and cool

Friend can write poems Friend can write books Friend is a praying woman she will have you shook

Friend is a mother your baby boy is smiling down from heaven

Friend is a hairstylist Friend can do a bob Friend can do waves Friend can do a fade she can even crochet Friend is gone be a business owner Friend gone be a wife Friend gone have her a really good life

Oh yeah and did I mention my friend melanin and juicy fruit be drip, drip drippin

Friend been happy Friend been sad Friend been excited Friend been mad but friend know GOD so she good with all that

Friend is loyal friend gone be down till the end and that right there I don't even have to question

Tiriah A.L. She is the Shhh!!!

That is my S.I.S.T.E.R. and friend

Enough

Why was I not enough for my father to stay around?

Why was I not enough for the marriage to last?

Why was I not enough for that situationship?

Was I not worth the commitment?

Why couldn't they see that I was putting on a smile all the while dying inside just wanting to be loved

God spoke and said you are enough and worthy of love, but you do have to love yourself first

So, whenever you feel like you are not enough, remember that God made you and I in his own image and that one thing alone is more than **Enough!**

1219

1219 starring at the screen wondering what I will see. With a daughter that is almost 16 and a son that is almost 11 how the hell did this happen? Well, I know how it happen so let me stop "capping".

On 1219 when I looked down at the screen never thought I would see pregnancy

On 1219 I could not believe that abortion would be the first response when I announced my pregnancy

On 1219 I came to the realization that I would be facing this situation all on my own

But I was mistaken because the Highest power who sits on the throne was there to carry me on

On 1219 God has brought me another blessing

127

On 127 looking at the emergency room entrance gotta find out what is going on cause this pain is so intense

This being the longest ultrasound of my life, but never did I think twice after two successful pregnancies the 3rd bundle of joy wouldn't come to be

When the doctor came in and closed the curtains, I felt the tears hit my t-shirt 8 weeks at the time that life had to fly home to be with the most high

On 127 what I thought was a lost was a blessing. The most high had to bring me to this point to see my current situation.

I could hear him speak so clearly this is not the man that I have for you who's colors have changed and intentions so un pure. He doesn't want your mental or spiritual he only wants your physical. All his words are lies, and he tells you what you want to hear because he fears the day when you will wake up with a mind so clear. So, on 127 my sweet life went to heaven and that current situation is now my past with never a future in it.

Aunt Linda

Aunt Linda Oh how I remember us both being a Gemini. Your beautiful smile and fashionable style.

Health issues caused you not to work as much. Oh how I would pray that you were home when I got off the school bus.

Oh, how I remember sitting in a bedroom decorated in all pink just so we could watch T.V.

Now one thing about Aunt Linda she did not play but it all came from a loving place.

A brain aneurysm is what the doctor's called it to be I remember all the anxiety attacks when they announced you would not be coming back.

Oh, Aunt Linda how I miss you and love you so much, but I know that it is God that loved you first.

God saw fit for you to come home with him and rest in eternal peace. One thing I know he choose you as one of the angels to watch over me.

Anxiety

I cannot breathe, my stomach is in knots and I am shaking uncontrollably. What is this taking over me mentally, spiritually, and emotionally. This has the potential to damage my life permanently. Why is my heart pounding and racing? A good night's sleep is what I find myself chasing. Work, cook, clean, laundry, make sure everything is taken care of except for me. Never in a million years did I think it would be anxiety.

Healing

Healing is something I do not think I have ever done.
I have always ignored the elephant in the room
Now the elephant in the room has gotten so big that there is
    no space left for me to stand in it.
The outside wounds scratches and scrapes have healed fine.
But I have never taken the time to heal my heart and mind.
Healing is a process that cannot be warmed up in the microwave
    more than a day or two is what it will take.
Healing is something that happens from the inside out.
The path to healing is what we most worry about not know how
    it will turn out.
But I am here to tell you from experience healing is something
    that is greatly needed.

Forgiveness

This poem will not be some version of a sad song about me still holding on to past wrongs. Forgiveness is for me and not for you. Forgiveness is for me to smile Forgiveness is for me to be happy now. Forgiveness is for my brain to rewire Forgiveness is for me to elevate higher Forgiveness is for me to walk in my purpose Forgiveness is for my renewed confidence Forgiveness is for positive energy Forgiveness is for a new me Forgiveness is for me to put back on my crown Forgiveness is for me to walk with my head held high Forgiveness is for me to love myself completely Forgiveness is for my communication to be healthy Forgiveness is to receive the man God has for me Forgiveness is for me to understand my worth Forgiveness is for me to set standards Forgiveness is for me to give love Forgiveness is for me to accept love Forgiveness is for my transition Forgiveness is for me to be a better mother to my children Forgiveness is for my mind body and spirit

Communication

Communication is a big word that often intimidates us.

Communication is a verb. An action that we most often do not
act upon.

I was never given the blueprint on how this action is to be
performed.

Never an example of how not to yell, cuss, scream, or fuss.

I beg the questions do you find yourself talking at and not to
someone?

Non communication can suffocate, strangle, and squeeze the life
out of our interactions and relations with other humans.

Non communication is a tool best used as a defense mechanism
to guard ourselves from being vulnerable.

Just the idea alone is way too uncomfortable

God only knows what would happen if communication was a
normalized practice.

Truth

Truth as my momma used to say is not beating around the bush or sugar coating your words. If you are surrounded by a group of people that will not tell you the truth, then what does that say about you?

Some say they want to hear it but can't handle it.

Some would rather lie than to tell it.

Do you know how many years I spent running from the truth? Because the hardest thing to do was look in the mirror and examine who? Myself with only I to look back to.

Sometimes the truth is hard to find. Sometimes the truth can make you cry.

But now that I have taken the time to search, seek, and find my truth I encourage you to do the same.

Tell the truth, live in your truth, because if not it would only be a detriment to you.

Character

What makes up the character of you? How do you act in private when no one sees you? It is easy to put on in public but when you look in the mirror do you feel ugly? When was the last time you did the work to go beyond the surface? The pedicure manicure and new bag will not fix change or reconfigure your past The new clothes will not fill the void within your soul The new house and car will not make you healed and whole When you cry will Facebook and Instagram come to wipe your eyes? Do you live your life as God intended? or are you trying to be God and pass judgment? No matter how good you look on the outside and the material things you acquire it will carry no value if what you lack is character.

Complicated

Complicated is a very ambiguous word. When you say it's complicated what does that really mean? Do you stay leave or are you in between? Mother daughter business partner father son husband wife friendships and the like are all relationships that can be complicated. But let me ask you, what are you doing to Un-complicate things?

I don't know/ I am confused

I am so confused I don't know the next move. I don't know which road to take if it is stop or wait if it is real or fake. I am confused by your hesitation and my weakened feminine intuition. I don't want to pass off judgement and make invalid assumptions but I am trying to figure out why you pressed pause instead of play. I don't like the mental and emotional state that I am in today. Confusion has caused my sight to be blurry so I need you to be my clarity so I can regain my 20/20 vision. I don't know what to say when there is no message that you have relayed. Lay your cards upon this table and maybe my confusion will dissipate. Until then I guess the confusion will remain. As my momma used to say I don't know ain't got no home so please remember that after you hear this poem.

Yesterday

I won't waste your time because I would not want someone to waste mine. But on yesterday you wasted mine. I am a man of my word but on yesterday your words were no where to be found. I went to be bed feeling empty and numb inside. I am trying hard not to place you in a box with all my past relations but that is not easy to do when there is no communication. You say there are some things you need to figure out but you won't express to me what that is all about. Something in my gut does not feel right come on let me in don't shut me out like you did on yesterday. Father I pray that whatever he is going through you will guide him in the right way and even if we don't communicate keep him safe.

Unconditional Presence

Extra Extra read all about it! My love may be unconditional but my presence in your life is not. My presence is contingent on how you treat me and at this current point and time there is no mat here to wipe your feet. I have been the door mat but that ain't happening no more. If the shoe was on the other foot and I did not treat you like I actually gave a damn if you were in your right mind you would skedaddle and scram. Your words and actions have to be on the same wavelength. I am ready and willing but whether or not I stay is dependent upon you and and like I said my presence is not unconditional.

I am not

I am not your mother so it is not my job to raise you. I am not a broken little girl looking for a man to fill a void. I will not bare the wounds of your past trauma. I will not be a punching bag for you to take your frustrations out on. I am not a door mat for you to wipe your indiscretions on. I will not pay for the crimes of the last woman. So, take my advice as I have done and heal before you move on to the next one. Because if I am a healed and whole woman I am not going to entertain a grown little boy. This is Renae Speaks and I repeat I am not that one.

I am sorry

Just what is the meaning behind saying I am sorry? The word itself did not break your heart into a million pieces make you cry or cause you sleepless nights. The word itself did not cause stress and weight loss having you looking in the mirror thinking that you are not good enough. One, two, three, four, a five letter word cannot make up for how utterly disturbed I am by your actions. I will accept your apology but not for you, for me. However there is no need for us to speak. You have reached my voice-mail so leave a message after the beep.

Thoughts

Can you love me the way I am supposed to be? Can you supply me with mental stimulation before penetration? Can you be my soft place to land? Believe me I am not only asking you these questions I am also taking inventory of me. Can I love a man the way he is suppose to be? Can I be his peace? Can I be the quiet in the storm. Am I able to give love and also receive the love that you would give back to me. Am I able to communicate my wants needs and desires effectively. Am I truly able to give you all of me? Can friendship be the foundation that we build upon? Are you going to be a thief in the night or do you want to be here for a lifetime? Will you be the protector of my heart or are you here to bring chaos and destroy? I want to build together. I want to be that consistent motivation for you to walk in your God given purpose. I want you to be there when my poetry is published. I want you to be the special guest on my podcast. Although it will never be perfect I want us to see the value and worth in each other to continue to make it better. These are the thoughts that inhabit my mind everyday.

Vulnerable

I really do want to be vulnerable with you. To open up and give you all of me. My heart and my body says yes but then my mind steps in and says no no no you have been here before. You already know where this will go he will only leave you sad and alone.

I really do want to be vulnerable with you. I want to grant you entrance into my special space but what will you do? Once again, my mind steps in and says he will only leave you broken and confused.

I really do want to be vulnerable with you. I want to grow with you. I want to accomplish goals with you. I want to be in love with and make love to you.

I want you to drown in my ocean of wetness and let me swallow the cum cause it ain't no fun if I don't swallow the cum.

I want your heart beat to be the music I fall asleep to and my smile will be what you wake up to. I really want to be vulnerable with you. The only thing I need to know is do you want to be vulnerable with me too?

Time

It's been a long time since our minds have intertwined. It's been a long time since we laid our souls bare. It has been a long time since we had a conversation. It's been a long time since I looked into your eyes and could see what was on your mind. It's been a long time since we created a space for bonding and intimacy to see into each other and be at peace. It's been a long time since we simply made time so let's rewind and do all these things before we run out of time.

Someone

I want someone who's touch will silence my doubts and fears. Whose kiss will forever be a moment in time when our lips intertwine. I want someone who will take my heart in their hands and be willing to handle it with care. Someone who does not just want to connect with me on a physical level but will want to help me reach new levels. Someone who wants to see the God and Goddess in me. Someone who wants to see my soul smile. Someone who will make me happy for a lifetime.

LOVE

Love can be a funny thing with all the different emotions it can
bring.
Love can be a sunny day. Love can be a mother's hug.
Love can be a tender kiss on the forehead. Love can be an
afternoon walk in the park. Love can be someone holding you
close in the dark.
Love can make you cry. Love can make you laugh. Sometimes
love can really make you mad.
Love is supposed to be unconditional but you and I both know
we tend to throw that out the window.
Now do not get it twisted love is not crazy. Love is not abusive.
Love is not jealous. Love should never make you feel like
your worthless.
Love is supposed to build you up and take care with you heart.
Love is together and not apart.
Now out of all the things that love can be and all the emotions it
may bring the one thing we must do is love ourselves and
others too.

I say I say

I say I say a lot of things but my mind and my heart are on a different wave length. I say I would rather be lonely but it is driving me crazy. I say I don't want to get married again but I think about it daily. I say I don't want to talk but conversation is all I dream about. I say I am a home body but I really want to get out the house and go on a date because the 4 walls are closing in on me. I say that I am good but finding it hard to breath. I say I say a lot of things but love is what my mind body and soul really needs.

Into me see

Into me see my soul vibrant, colorful, and bold
Into me see my heart it has been damaged but beating strong
Into me see my eyes dark yet bright and reflecting life
Into me see a proud mother who loves her children like no other
Into me see the daughter who would not be the woman she is
    today without her mother
Into me see the voice that was developed by singing in the church
    choir
Into me see my intelligent mind that can be naughty at the same
    time
Into me see the shy yet talkative girl that just wants to be loved
Into me see the strong and determined queen that has made it
    through so many things
But, in order to really see me there must be space for intimacy

You

Hello You yeah I am talking to You. Hello You yeah I am talking to You. You will know that intimacy is not just physical You can also penetrate my mental You will caress my soul and make love to my mind before our bodies ever intertwine. You will have purpose and be intentional when seeking out this beautiful Black Queen because he knows he has to come correct when stepping up on my scene You will be funny, smart, and ambitious You will be on a mission yeah I said a mission to find what he been missing You will like how I just spoke all these things into existence You will know that I am the cream of the crop the warm baked apple pie with the cherry on top I don't know the who, what, and when of meeting You but until then this joint right here is specifically for the one and only

YOU

You-Part 2

You, You yeah I am talking to You I had to cone thru with a part 2

You will know that material things don't really mean a thing You will know that there is no price tag on intangible things You will want to give me his time You will actually want to have conversation and take me out in public You will have a vision of what his life will be like with me in it no doubt You will not be indecisive You will be a MAN in every sense of the word he will match his actions with his words You will know that the continued pursuit of his dreams and goals will not only help himself but our relationship to grow You will love GOD and his momma You will not be down with all that DRAMA

Well, that is all for now Mr. You I just had to come thru with a few more words for this….

PART 2

In a relationship

I am in a relationship with me. I am in a relationship with my peace. I am in a relationship with positive energy. I am in a relationship with my creator. I am in a relationship with my healing. I am in a relationship with my growth. I am in a relationship with my goals. I am in a relationship with financial stability. I am in a relationship with my new life journey. I am in a relationship where I am learning to love ME. Relationship status updated from single to in a relationship with SELF.

SELF love is the best love.

Potential

Push push past your potential. All the ideas, thoughts, dreams, and goals locked inside the tiniest corner of your mind is what you should seek to find. Push past the potential to be greater in the future. Do not seek to become that speak into existence that you already are that. Push past that 1 song to an album. Push past the social media live to a podcast. Push past being the fashion buyer to the fashion designer. Push past the GED to the college degree. Push past the drawing on a piece of paper to an art gallery. Push past your mind to your spirituality. Push past your emotion and get your chakras in line. Push past start to the finish line. So, push, push past your potential because that is what the most high placed you in this universe for.

I cannot wait

I cannot wait I cannot wait God is telling me girl you cannot wait. The gifts and talents that you have can inspire a girl or maybe the world. I cannot wait to write another poem or sing another song. I cannot wait on my dreams and goals I must be brave courageous and bold. I cannot continue to sit in the dark and let the enemy pull me under. I cannot continue to place limitations on myself that is only a detriment to my mental health. The young man standing on the ledge thinking he would be better off dead cannot wait. The young girl sitting in the doctor's office wondering whether to terminate her offspring cannot wait. The marriage on the brink of divorce cannot wait. That abusive partner cannot wait. The business plans you have cannot wait. That college degree cannot wait. The son with no father cannot wait. The motherless daughter cannot wait. That nonprofit organization cannot wait. The chef that wants to open a restaurant cannot wait. Letting go of hate cannot wait. Loving yourself cannot wait. So, therefore I cannot wait and pled with you to move with the same haste. Because together our voices gifts and talents could inspire and change the fate of some of the scenarios that I have spoke about on this date.

Calling

Something is calling me.

My mind does not yet understand, and my eyes have not seen.

But, like the softest whisper it is calling me in my sleep and dreams.

Like a present not yet unraveled, I question what road to travel.

What purpose does God have written for my life?

In what place and on what stage am I to be. The answers to these questions are what I believe is calling me. I will continue to seek and maybe I will sleep peacefully when I am living my purpose in reality.

Shine a light

Shine a light in a dark place shine a light on your beautiful face

Shine a light on depression shine a light on that toxic relationship

Shine a light on God's grace and mercy shine a light on social injustice

Shine a light on our nation shine a light on the Motherland where my ancestors came from

Shine a light on that Sunday dinner for all to see shine a light on that Red Velvet cake recipe

Shine a light on the smoothie you made shine a light on the vitamins you take

Shine a light on your dreams shine a light on your makeup routine shine a light on your journey to becoming a QUEEN

Shine a light on the KINGS who are fathers taking the time to raise their sons and daughters

Shine a light on that job promotion shine a light on the business you just opened

Shine a light on your engagement shine a light on that newborn baby

Shine a light so bright as to inspire and never dim it down because it is needed and required.

Speak

Speak to my soul it has not been left out in the cold

Speak to my heart its ok to find the key to the lock

Speak to my mind so it can relax and stop running a million miles at a time

Speak to my life it will get better in God's time

Speak to my children let then know how much momma love them

Speak to my family I will love yall till the death of me

Speak to my future that is one I will continue to nurture

Speak to my daddy I forgive you for not being there

Speak to ME so that I can be the pure, and unadulterated, best version of myself and give that to somebody

But the only way to do that is to Speak!

Use it

Let's use what we have to make it past any obstacle that stands in our path. Use the negative for positive. Use the sadness for happiness, use the brokenness for healing, use the no to get a yes, use the fear to build confidence, use illness to bring awareness, use chaos to bring about peace, use dysfunction to bring about a new routine. use darkness to create a new energy whatever it may be, use it to make sure the mind, body, and spirit are as healed and whole as can be.

New

New for me, new for you. A new beginning is raw and unfamiliar at its core. Something that we have not yet given birth to. A new friendship, a new car, a new house, a new love, a new life. Whatever the new pertains to, don't let that spark a scary feeling within you. New is the morning sunrise. New is a walk on the beach with the water lapping at your feet. New is the smile on your face when a new interaction takes place. New for me, new for you now it is time to give birth to new.

This BLACK

This black was created in melanin because as the sun does it is supposed to keep shine, shine, shinning.

This black is handsome, beautiful, courageous, and crazy.

This black is loving, intelligent, persistent, and committed.

This black is Queen. This black is a mother This black is King. This black is a father.

This black is an entrepreneur. This black is a barber. This black is a singer, songwriter, and even an author.

This black is in the board room meetings and at the drive thru window.

This black is proud yet humble.

So, for all the reasons mentioned above and thousands more this black will be celebrated everyday because the last time I recall our ancestors spent more than the month of February in bondage and slavery.